Whitney Museum
of American Art

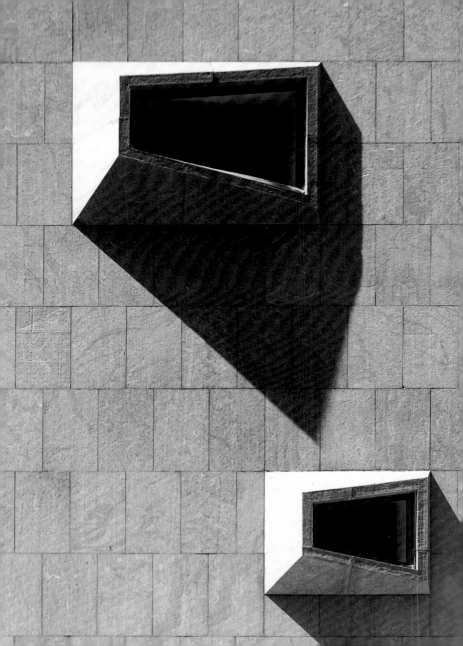

Whitney Museum of American Art

Photographs by Ezra Stoller

With new photography by Jeff Goldberg
Preface by Maxwell L. Anderson
Introduction by K. Michael Hays

building **blocks**

Princeton Architectural Press • New York

The BUILDING BLOCKS series presents the masterworks of modern architecture through the iconic images of acclaimed architectural photographer Ezra Stoller.

Contents

Preface

Maxwell L. Anderson

THE WHITNEY MUSEUM's home stands defiantly apart from identifiable trends of twentieth-century New York architecture, and has accordingly not aged since its opening in the fall of 1966. At the time, the vertiginous International Style glass towers rising in midtown seemed in sync both with the futuristic optimism of the recent 1964 New York World's Fair, and with the sameness of "the organization man" pilloried by William Hollingsworth Whyte in his 1956 book of that title. The Whitney's blocky new building stood the status quo on its head, using the vernacular of Mesopotamian antiquity—the ziggurat—to question the received architectural wisdom of the contemporary era. It still does. Not out of spite or ridicule, but out of a questioning spirit—that quintessentially American trait that rejects conformity for its own sake.

When it opened, the building had a formidable resonance for me, a young Manhattanite with a rebellious nature. Decades later, entering the Whitney I find the architectural experience as rewarding as it was on my first visit, because the Breuer building is brilliantly flexible in its galleries, elegant beyond compare in its spare granite, concrete, and slate palette, and oddly severe but playful in its visual metaphors. While other twentieth-century museum buildings in New York may stray toward the quirky or the generic, the Whitney winks through its polygonal windows at passersby, seduces them to enter, and rewards each visitor with its ageless simplicity. Those of us privileged enough to work in it endure its modest size but revel in its boldness and its integrity in the face of fleeting fashion.

Maxwell L. Anderson is Director,
Whitney Museum of American Art

Introduction

K. Michael Hays

THE WHITNEY MUSEUM OF AMERICAN ART was destined to be a landmark. When it opened, in September 1966, architect Marcel Breuer was at the height of his career. Having left a teaching position at Harvard's Graduate School of Design for New York in 1946, he had amassed a body of work that included educational, industrial, religious, and commercial buildings, as well as a series of highly praised residential projects and community plans. His was a late-modern architecture that was sculptural, brooding, and slightly enigmatic, more open to monumentality and symbolism than its predecessors— even if ambivalently so—but still committed to clarity of structure and function. The Whitney was, moreover, the first new museum in Manhattan since Frank Lloyd Wright's Guggenheim, which opened in 1959, and the first devoted entirely to American art, with an emphasis on contemporary work. Officially begun in 1930, transformed out of the lively and liberal Whitney Studio Club, the museum was initially housed in three remodeled townhouses on West

Marcel Breuer at the Whitney Museum in 1966.

Eighth Street. In 1949, the trustees of the Museum of Modern Art donated part of their land on West Fifty-fourth Street to the Whitney, and in 1954 a new building was opened on that site. In 1963, the museum, under the directorship of Lloyd Goodrich and with a budget of six million dollars (including money for land), chose Breuer and his associate architect, Hamilton Smith, to design their new 76,830-square-foot home. Breuer's new building, on the corner of Madison Avenue and Seventy-fifth Street, would not only triple the exhibition and administrative space of the museum, but give it, for the first time, its own identity.

"What should a museum look like, a museum in Manhattan?" Breuer asked himself, pondering the question of identity and symbolism.* "Surely it should work, it should house its requirements, but what is its relationship to the New York landscape? What does it express, what is its architectural message?"[1] Imagine Breuer about to set pen to paper. What bank of ideas had he to draw from? When he'd needed architectural symbolism before, in Minnesota's Saint John's Abbey (1953–61), for example, he'd had precedents more time-tested to start from. He noted that "although the church may be a new sensation to the eye, its architectural concept does resemble in some ways those of religious buildings of the Middle Ages and the Classic period." There was the bell tower that could be framed in raw concrete and set out in the remote landscape. And there was the certainty of structure. "Whether stone lintels on stone columns are employed, or Roman or Gothic arches, whether dome, barrel vault, or folded plates of concrete, church architecture, at its best, is always identical with the structural logic of the enclosure."[2] But here, on a tiny 100 x 125-

---

* Breuer's statement, "Comments at the Presentation of the Whitney Museum Project," from which this quote is drawn, is reprinted in its entirety on pages 81–4 of this volume.

foot lot on the corner of an increasingly commercialized Madison Avenue, facing a deep hole already excavated before his commission, Breuer found little in his experience of immediate help. A few things, however, were clear to him:

> It is easier to say first what [the museum] should not look like. It should not look like a business or office building, nor should it look like a place of light entertainment. Its form and its material should have identity and weight in the neighborhood of fifty-story skyscrapers, of mile-long bridges, in the midst of the dynamic jungle of our colorful city….It should transform the vitality of the street into the sincerity and profundity of art.[3]

Breuer's musings, bland at first gloss, take on an urgency in their historical context, for the forging of an identity, especially an identity for art, was anything but easy in mid-1960s Manhattan. And it was especially difficult on Madison Avenue, seat of the advertising industry. American affluence was the motor of a spectacular consumer society that produced frantic waves of products and images, in the process threatening to diminish the object of art to the status of commodity. Doubts about whether the "profundity of art"—a force, however feeble, against the processes of commodification—could be mobilized to create a critical distance from the numbing whir of business and commerce were registered again and again by the critics who reviewed Breuer's building in the press. Peter Blake, for one, knew who the enemy was, and what its architecture looked like:

> Here on Madison Avenue, Breuer is about to mount a massive attack against those who have made the name of this avenue synonymous with their racket. The new Whitney will be art's answer to the huckster: where the ad agencies operate behind

flimsy glass walls, the Whitney will be wrapped in concrete faced with granite; where the commercial ziggurats push the pedestrian off the sidewalk, the Whitney will invite him in; and where the right-side-up ziggurats down the avenue now symbolize the huckster's perversion of art, the Whitney's upside-down monolith may become a powerful symbol of art "sailing against the currents of its time."[4]

And so Breuer's statement that "It is easier to say first what it should not look like." It should not look like the expanded bureaucracy that had appropriated and stamped so much of postwar architecture with spread-sheet anonymity (in particular the stepped International Style buildings along Madison Avenue, products of Manhattan zoning laws that encouraged repeated setbacks). And it should not look like the products of the consumerist popular culture that surrounded it. If nothing else, the Whitney Museum was to be a refuge for *Art*.

We are led, then, to consider one of the fundamental problems of modern architecture: how is the negative to be constructed in practice? How can a building that is historically and culturally enmeshed in a system represent a resistance to that same system? It is here that the photographs of Ezra Stoller come to our aid. Stoller's photographs of freestanding buildings often employ a one-point perspective with an exact center and a foreground-to-distance thrust that at once firmly places the viewer and draws him into the sweep of the image, creating an exhilaration conjoined with certainty.[5] A similar technique is used in his view of the Whitney's fourth-floor gallery, the museum's largest. Rather than ground and sky in the upper and lower registers, there are floor and ceiling; and rather than a freestanding building, there are sculptures, paintings, and, at the center, Breuer's window onto Madison Avenue, itself flattened by the picture plane into two dimensions. In the left foreground, the arms of an Alexander Calder mobile function like the foliage of a tree framing one of Stoller's canonical outdoor shots. And the certainty of the one-point perspective now conveys a stability and a manageability of space. What is in fact a huge gallery, nearly 17½-feet-high, is made to feel almost residential in scale without seeming petty in purpose—a striking combination of grandness and domesticity. The photograph of the Gertrude Vanderbilt Whitney Gallery (pages 48–9), which appears like nothing so much as the benefactor's living room, confirms the coupling. Stoller understood that, for Breuer, the greatness of art was best apprehended in a parlor, for like the space of the parlor, the aesthetic experience is at once social and personal.

This domestication cannot be overemphasized, as it was one of Breuer's primary tactics for ensuring the museum's difference from the commercial street and its hucksters, and of guaranteeing a continuation of the Whitney's radical and committed past. For the early institution was radical (at least insofar as it was a direct attack on the academic jury system—in the Whitney Studio Club, there were no juries, each artist-member could select his or her own piece to exhibit, and membership was open to all) and that radicality was bound up with its domesticity. John Morris Dixon said in 1966 that the character of the new Whitney was "more like that of a private mansion than of an anonymous public treasury."[6] And a writer in the *AIA Journal*, thinking back to the opening of the Whitney, confirmed something like an estrangement effect for the interiors:

> My own recollections of the building in its first few years (reinforced by another look at Ezra Stoller's classic photographs of the opening exhibition) remind me of how much like a club or a private mansion it was at first. The people who conceived this original design must have been thinking of serving that small

group of aficionados who before the 1960s were devoted to American art….[The galleries] were intended to resemble and be used like the intimate rooms of the earlier buildings of the museum.[7]

In its interiors, the Whitney maintains a discrete distance between art and street, but outside things are far less subtle. The Whitney is a defensive structure, and when it opened few critics failed to see it as some kind of fortress. Blake called it a "*Kunstbunker,*" and an editorial in *Art News* described it as "a black Crusader Castle among the tearooms and boutiques of Madisonia."[8] Breuer bracketed the site with concrete walls and a moat to fend off the encroachments of the glass-walled skyscrapers sure to come (they never arrived, preservationist sentiments changing as they did). From this space, the building emerged. And *emerge* is the right word, for the site seems to have been cracked open, allowing the Whitney's Cyclopean head to appear and then focus its attention on the apotropaic purpose of Breuer's summons.

Anthropomorphic though it may be, Breuer did not arrive at a figurative architecture that easily (I use the term *figure* here to suggest Breuer's attempt to represent a complex set of values through an emblematic, expressive architectural form, a form that nevertheless remains true to modernist ideals of abstraction). Even the late work of the architect, an ex-Bauhausler, perpetuates the Bauhaus legacy of modularity and mass production (his later works are famous for their precast concrete panels). And the Whitney, too, begins not with a figure but with an easily reproducible geometric form—a cube—which then becomes a series of nested or overlapping square blocks telescoped diagonally upward. It is a positivist's attempt at a significant profile, as if a programmatic requirement had distorted the building's geometry, pushing out the volumes of its own accord. It is not figurative *per se*, but produces the effect of figure with the alibi of function. It is a tilt at the popular culture Breuer perceived as threatening.

Then there is the reference to Wright's Guggenheim, the Whitney's most immediate predecessor and surely the most obvious and viable example of what a museum in Manhattan "should look like." Critics at the time didn't miss the nod to Wright—more than one called the Whitney a squared-off Guggenheim—and the crib could not have been totally unconscious on Breuer's part. In a 1945 interview in *Time* magazine, Wright declared that the "basic idea" of the Guggenheim had come from the ancient ziggurat, which he then inverted, creating an "optimistic ziggurat." Surely Wright's sanction of this reference aided Breuer in his effort to find an architectural form adequate to a museum's representational demands.[9]

In a series of photographs of the front facade, Stoller seems to search the building for the right balance of monumental permanence and, especially in the shots with strong shadows under the stacked volumes, a sense of hovering substantiality. His search is not accidental. Breuer wanted his ziggurat to appear weightless. Ever since his early designs for chairs—the Wassily (1925), the Cesna (1928)—he had found satisfaction in the use of industrial materials to make the body appear to float in midair. At the Whitney, he set himself the even more daunting task of levitating a monolithic building, for in the juxtaposition between mass and buoyancy was further expressive power. "Today's structure in its most expressive form is hollow below and substantial on top—just the reverse of the pyramid," said Breuer. "It represents a new epoch in the history of man, the realization of one of his oldest ambitions: the defeat of gravity."[10]

So the Whitney is not exactly a work of figurative architecture, but something between figuration and abstraction—or better, an abstract figure. The cube is taken from the Bauhausler's repository of known forms, and the symbolic ziggurat comes through a set of

8

swerves and detours—the swerve out of pure functionalism, the detour through Wright, the attempt to find an expression adequate for a refuge for art in a culture that can consume and degrade any expression—that wind up lurching toward an authenticity of representation that cannot be represented directly. The museum building, by dint of its cultural status and specific historical moment, had to carry a message that pure form alone could not shoulder. The shape of the Whitney is the certainty of form inflected by the cultural necessity of figure; the shape stands for "the sincerity and profundity of art" that might still emerge against an image culture threatening to push it back underground.

The art historian Michael Fried, writing in 1966 about Frank Stella's paintings of that same year, found in those paintings an investigation of shape as a medium that could "compel conviction" and have the "power to hold, to stamp itself out." This is precisely what Breuer was after, and for many of the same reasons. Fried argues that Stella's focus on shape was a historically driven development in modernism, a reaction to the threat of "literalness" exhibited by such minimalist sculptors as Donald Judd and Larry Bell. To Fried, the reductive boxes created by Judd and Bell lacked any transcendent quality, and were an abdication of art's obligation to differentiate and distance itself from quotidian objects.[11] Breuer was similarly dissatisfied with architecture he perceived as lacking any transcendent quality: architecture that gave in to the temptations of commodity lust or that abandoned to glibness any effort at resistance and willingly appropriated the forms of consumerism—the photographic advertisement, the billboard, the "vitality of the street" left untransformed.

Recognizing the search for a transcendent architecture and the implicit rejection of popular culture as the soft underbelly of Breuer's purpose, in 1976 Robert Venturi appropriated Breuer's museum to make one of his most revealing critiques of late-modern architecture.

LEFT: STEPHEN SHORE; RIGHT: JERRY L. THOMPSON

LEFT: *Photocutout of Hiram Powers's* Greek Slave *placed on the Whitney canopy by Robert Venturi for the 1976 exhibition* 200 Years of American Sculpture. RIGHT: *Banners by Kay Rosen on the Whitney facade during the* 2000 Biennial *exhibition once again make the building a sign.*

Commissioned to design the exhibition *200 Years of American Sculpture* at the Whitney, he placed a 28-foot-high, Caesar's Palace-inspired photographic cutout of Hiram Powers's 1847 statue *Greek Slave* atop Breuer's entrance canopy, its perspective adjusted to account for the hump at Seventy-first Street. This Vegas-style sign of low-brow, popular culture—which Breuer's blank-screen facade had tried so hard to rebuff—was a direct challenge to the architect's attempt at profundity. Though sticks and stones couldn't hurt Breuer's bunker, mockery had a certain effect. Here, it can at least help us pick out what Breuer most feared and tried to defend against.

Stoller understood the Whitney's shape was itself a statement about the transcendent power of form, and he also understood the building's talismanic function. His photograph of the lower portion of the building—its profile honed almost too sharp for stone, cut out of the shadows and occupying half of the composition—sets that profile against the street as its other. The disjunction of scale—the building impossibly close and big—separates worlds and worldviews that, in fact, reside in the same space. Both building and street bear the stigmata of consumerism, as Theodor Adorno might have said—the building in its defensive distortions, the street in its laissez-faire variety and vitality. Both must respond to capital's demands for a representational logic that, in the ensuing decade, coalesced into the "cultural dominant" that we now call postmodernism. The two registers of the photograph are the torn halves of an emergent postmodernity to which they do not yet add up.[12]

Finally, there are Breuer's idiosyncratic windows. Rumor has it that Breuer wanted no windows at all, artificial lighting being sufficient and, to him, preferable for the display of paintings. Some critics found the windows arbitrary or capricious, but they are not arbitrarily placed, each being dutifully centered on a gallery space. It is hard, nevertheless, to square them with Breuer's tactics for the rest of the building. The museum's profile can be rationalized as a concession to programmatic requirements and a transformation of a purely geometric condition, but the windows are neither. And Breuer had used trapezoidal windows before. At St. Francis de Sales Church (1961–67), roughly the same shape bulges out from the otherwise continuous skin of the sanctuary to make room for a chapel, and then is repeated at a much smaller size and stuck on an enclosing wall to house the stations of the cross. Shapes not so different had resulted from the industrially produced, stamped concrete panels Breuer loved for their sculptural effects of light and shade. But in these cases such plastic effects were pleasant gratuities laid over the fundamental requirements of program and procedures of fabrication and assembly. At the Whitney, they cannot be thus rationalized, so critics have resorted to anthropomorphic metaphors: "beetle-browed windows," "leering bug-eyes," "mechanical pincers," "eyes on art," warts on the skin of the giant stony toad. Breuer himself called them "eyebrows." "They look symbolic," said one critic, and I think he is right if he meant they look as if they are trying to be symbolic but are not quite sure what symbolic looks like.[13] Faced with the need for depth, for aura, Breuer resorted to forms that had been successful for him in the past. But the result is garbled, a forcing of the building's skin to become physiognomic where a taciturn but confident consistency of surface should have sufficed. It is poignant and somewhat ironic that Stoller choose to encapsulate Breuer in his problematic window in his classic portrait of the architect.

I like to imagine that the doors to Breuer's new museum were flung open just as the bindings were glued onto Robert Venturi's *Complexity and Contradiction in Architecture.* Though Venturi never even bothers to mention Breuer by name in the book, entire chapters might have been written just to irritate the old master. His glib eclecticism is nothing if not an affront to Breuer's lifelong dedication to straightforward, functionally determined solutions, prefabricated building components, and a design method modeled on a simplified view of science. "It is significant," writes Vincent Scully in his introduction to *Complexity and Contradiction,* "that Venturi's ideas have so far stirred the bitterest resentment among the more academic-minded of the Bauhaus generation—with its utter lack of irony, its spinsterish disdain for the popular culture but shaky grasp on any other, its incapacity to deal with monumental scale, its lip-service to technology, and its preoccupation with a rather prissily puristic aesthetic."[14]

The point of which is just the reminder that while Venturi now stands for the set of architectural strategies, forms, and perceptual conventions we have come to call postmodern, the Whitney stands in the same complex of historical and social conditions that enabled, even demanded, postmodernism's emergence. It is telling that, in his three alternative schemes for an extensive addition to the Whitney (1981–92), Michael Graves seized on the latent figuration in Breuer's building, pushing it across a threshold to an overtly representational composition. Graves's project (much more sympathetic to Breuer than Venturi's intervention) skewered the Whitney with an imaginary architectural time line reaching from antiquity through the Enlightenment and straight to the heart of 1980s high postmodernism. But as if to confirm the contradictory perceptions the Whitney makes possible, there was enough of a public outcry from those who would "save" a purely modernist Whitney from this postmodern subsumption that, finally, not one of Graves's alternatives was approved.

Though I suspect Breuer would have understood his work as having been placed in an altogether different world from postmodernism, his building is marked in its fundamental forms by the contradictory cultural forces at work when it was produced. These forces seem to have pushed him to exceed modernism's standard references to function, structure, and technology; they demanded that he push his architecture to find its way back to representation, to signs that stood for things outside themselves, that he find his way to figure

NOTES

1. Marcel Breuer, "Comments at the Presentation of the Whitney Museum Project," 12 November 1963, reprinted on pages 81–4 of this volume.

2. Marcel Breuer, "Structure…Symbol" (notes referring to St. John's Abbey Church, 20 September 1961), in *Tician Papachristou, Marcel Breuer: New Buildings and Projects* (New York: Praeger, 1970), 12.

3. Breuer, "Comments," 81.

4. Peter Blake, "How the Museum Works," *Art in America* 34, no. 5 (September–October 1966): 27. The internal quotation is from a speech by President John F. Kennedy. For another view on the Whitney and consumerism, see Michael Brawne, "The New Whitney: The Building," *Art Forum* 3, no. 5 (November 1966): 46–55.

5. See William S. Saunders, *Modern Architecture: Photographs by Ezra Stoller* (New York: Abrams, 1990).

6. John Morris Dixon, "The Whitney: Big for Its Size," *Architectural Forum* 125, no. 2 (September 1966): 84.

7. Bernard P. Spring, "Evaluation: The Whitney Suffers from Success," *AIA Journal* (September 1978): 43.

8. *Art News* 65, no. 6 (October 1966): 29.

9. See chapter x, "The Guggenheim Museum's Logic of Inversion," of Neil Levine's *The Architecture of Frank Lloyd Wright* (Princeton, NJ: Princeton University Press, 1996). The *Time* interview is quoted on page 354.

10. Breuer, quoted in Brawne, "The New Whitney," 46.

11. Michael Fried, "Shape as Form: Frank Stella's Irregular Polygons" (1966), in *Art and Objecthood* (Chicago, The University of Chicago Press, 1998), 77.

12. The reference here is to Theodor Adorno's 1936 letter to Walter Benjamin in which he casts their two positions—Adorno's for autonomous art, Benjamin's for a productivist reproducibility—as "torn halves of an integral freedom, to which however they do not add up." Adorno, et al., *Aesthetics and Politics* (London: Verso, 1977), 123.

13. James T. Burns, *Progressive Architecture* (October 1966): 238; Charles Jencks, *Late-Modern Architecture* (New York: Rizzoli, 1980), 76; Sydney LeBlanc, *Whitney Guide to Twentieth-Century American Architecture* (New York: Whitney Library, 1993), 128; John Morris Dixon, "The Whitney," 81.

14. Vincent Scully, introduction to Robert Venturi, *Complexity and Contradiction in Architecture* (New York: The Museum of Modern Art, 1966), 15.

Plates

19

26

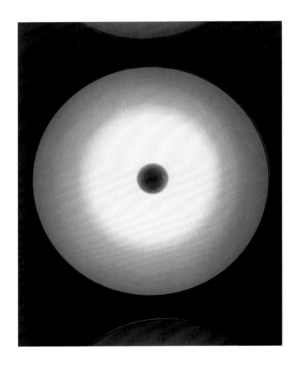

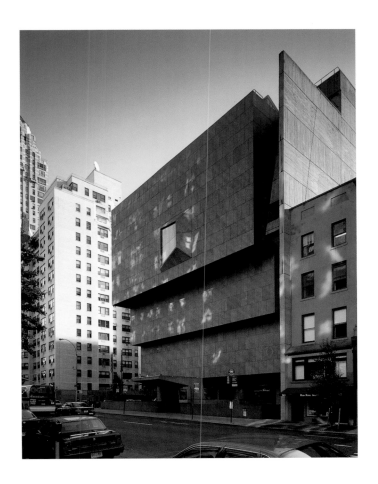

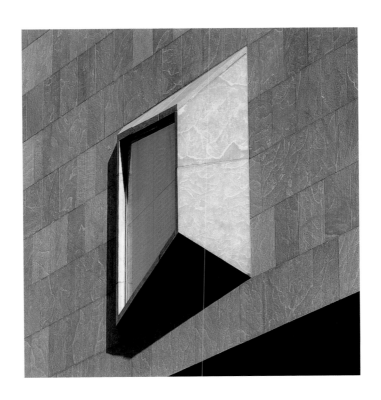

Drawings & Plans

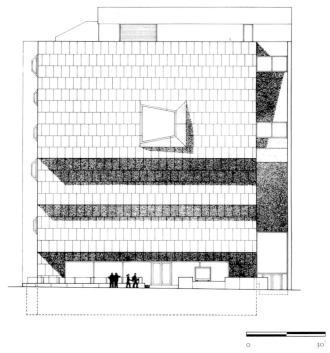

Madison Avenue elevation

0   30'

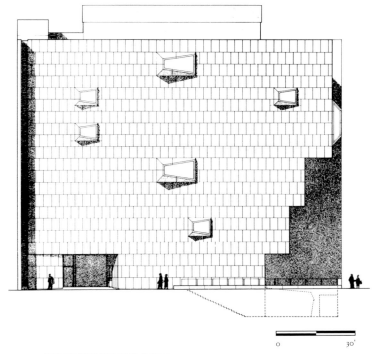

Seventy-fifth Street elevation

0   30'

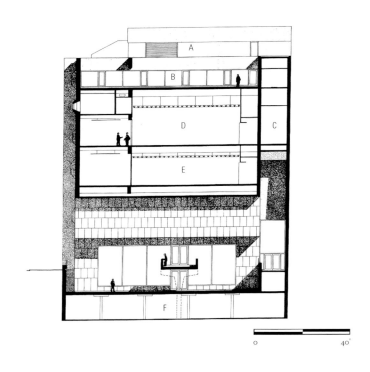

0   40'

Section cut north-south across upper floors

A. MECHANICAL	D. FOURTH FLOOR	E. THIRD FLOOR
B. OFFICES	GALLERY	GALLERY
C. SERVICE		F. BASEMENT

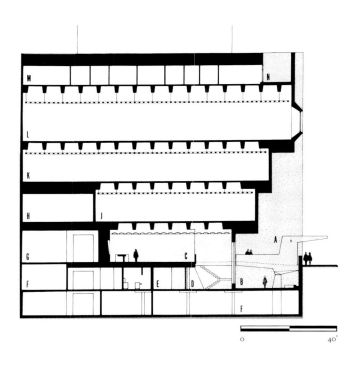

0   40'

Section cut east-west

A. ENTRANCE BRIDGE

B. SCULPTURE COURT

C. LOBBY

D. SCULPTURE GALLERY

E. CAFETERIA

F. PAINTING STORAGE

G. LOADING DOCK

H. AUDITORIUM

J. SECOND FLOOR
   GALLERY

K. THIRD FLOOR
   GALLERY

L. FOURTH FLOOR
   GALLERY

M. OFFICES

N. ROOF TERRACE

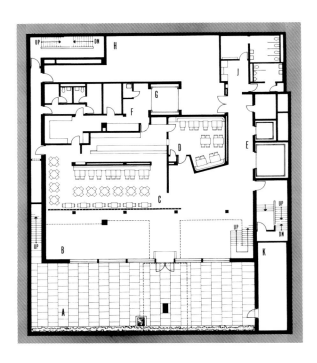

o   30'

Lower Floor plan

A. SCULPTURE COURT   D. FRIENDS' LOUNGE   H. SCULPTURE STORAGE

B. SCULPTURE GALLERY   E. ELEVATORS   J. REST ROOMS

C. CAFETERIA   F. KITCHEN AND STAFF   K. STORAGE

                                G. FREIGHT ELEVATOR

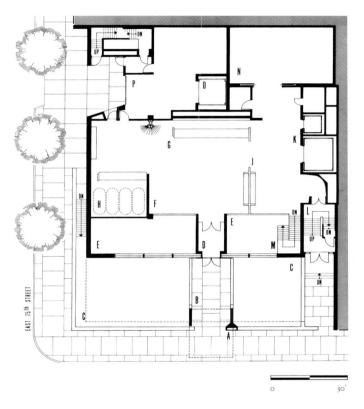

Ground Floor plan

A. EXHIBIT NOTICES

B. ENTRANCE BRIDGE

C. SCULPTURE COURT

D. VESTIBULE

E. WELL TO SCULPTURE
   GALLERY

F. LOBBY

G. INFORMATION &
   SALES DESK

H. COAT ROOM

J. ENTRY GATE

K. ELEVATORS

L. STAIRWELL

M. STAIR TO LOWER
   LEVEL

N. GALLERY

O. FREIGHT ELEVATOR

P. LOADING DOCK

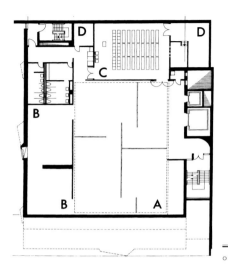

Second Floor plan

A. FLEXIBLE EXHIBITION
    SPACE
B. GALLERY
C. AUDITORIUM
D. STORAGE

o   25'

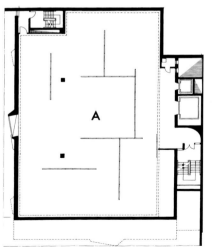

Third Floor plan

A. GALLERY

o   25'

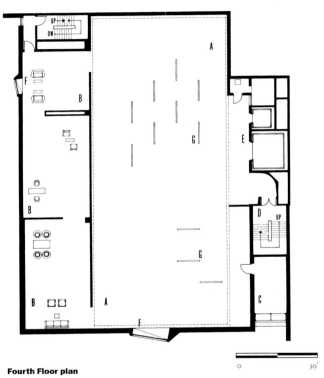

Fourth Floor plan

A. FLEXIBLE GALLERY
WITH MOVABLE
PARTITIONS

B. PERMANENT
GALLERY

C. RESTORATION LAB

D. STAIRWELL

E. ELEVATORS

F. WINDOW

G. MOVABLE
PARTITIONS

O   30'

Marcel Breuer at the Whitney Museum in 1966.

Architect's Statement

Marcel Breuer

*Comments at the Presentation of the Design of the Whitney Museum
Project to the Museum's Board of Trustees, 12 November 1963*

WHAT SHOULD A museum look like, a museum in Manhattan?
Surely it should work, it should fulfill its requirements, but what is its
relationship to the New York landscape? What does it express, what is
its architectural message?

It is easier to say first what is should *not* look like. It should not
look like a business or office building, nor should it look like a place
of light entertainment. Its form and its material should have identity
and weight in the neighborhood of fifty-story skyscrapers, of mile-
long bridges, in the midst of the dynamic jungle of our colorful city.
It should be an independent and self-relying unit, exposed to history,
and at the same time it should have visual connection to the street, as
it deems to the housing for twentieth-century art. It should transform
the vitality of the street into the sincerity and profundity of art.

The conception of the project shows a sunken sculpture court
between the sidewalk and the building—spanned over by the

Breuer at the Whitney in 1966.

entrance bridge and it shows the Madison Avenue glass front of the lobby and sculpture gallery: contact with the passersby. While the inverted pyramid of the building mass calls attention to the museum and to its special dedication, the mass is surfaced with a most durable, retiring and serene material: a warm gray granite, rather dark. The structure, reaching out high over the sculpture yard, does not stop the daylight and the west sun, and receives the visitor before he actually enters the interior of the building. One sees the sunken yard and its sculptures from the sidewalk and the entrance bridge. Also one sees the lobby and the sculpture gallery through the glass walls. To emphasize the completeness of the architectural form, the granite facades on both streets are separated from the neighboring fronts: an attempt to solve the inherent problem of a corner building which otherwise could easily look like a quarter part of something. The project transforms the building into a unit, an element, a nucleus, and lends it a direction toward Madison Avenue. The overall granite facing, homogeneous, extending out and over toward Madison Avenue, reaching down into the sunken garden with openings that grow out of the surface, with the modulations of the Madison Avenue gap between it and the neighboring buildings, with the granite parapet along the sidewalk, and with the structural concrete form of the bridge—all this is to form the building itself as a sculpture. However, a sculpture with rather functional requirements:

1. Simplicity and background-character of the gallery spaces with the visitors' attention reserved to the exhibits; flexibility of these spaces. Solutions for these demands are offered by rectangular and uncluttered large gallery spaces, interrupted by no columns or beams, partitioned by means of easily interchangeable floor-to-ceiling panels; a ceiling grid that permits and promotes this interchangeability, including that of the lighting; all walls and panels are light gray, the concrete ceiling a related gray, and the split-slate floors another related darker gray.

2. The floor area needed is about six to seven times greater than the site. This makes top-lighted gallery spaces impossible, aside from the fact that daylight would be reflected and colored by the tall apartment block buildings opposite. Windows or exterior glass areas would be disturbing and would reduce gallery hanging space. Consequently, our building has controlled mechanical ventilation, heated or cooled, and controlled, adjustable lighting in all gallery spaces. We recognize that lighting is probably the most important single element of a museum.

Windows have lost their justification for existence in this building; only a very few remain, and only to establish a contact with the outside. These few openings, free from the strict requirements of ventilation and lighting, can now be formed and located in a free and less inhibited fashion: as an architectural contrast to the strength of the main building lines.

3. It seems that large open gallery spaces with interchangeable partitions have to be watched, otherwise the general impression will be too clinical, to remote from the role of art. To avoid this danger—the danger of *l'art pour l'art museum-art*—we suggest for the galleries rather unsophisticated, close to earth materials: roughly

textured concrete ceilings; split-slate floors; flat-painted, canvas-covered walls. Furthermore, the design includes a number of smaller, noninterchangeable rooms of definite decoration and furnishings. Painting and sculpture can be shown in those in surroundings similar to a home or a place of assembly, or an office or a public building, theater, restaurant, school. The auditorium on the second gallery level will serve as an exhibition space.

4. While the average gallery height is 12 feet 9 inches clear, the top gallery height is 17 feet 6 inches. This is in consideration of the increasing size of contemporary painting. The sculpture gallery is double-story high, according to the wishes of a number of artists I talked to about this.

5. A maximum number of offices and the conference room have natural light. They are visually connected to the roof terraces, by means of glass walls. High parapet walls lend these terraces and the offices complete privacy, and their own atmosphere of concentration indoors and outdoors.

Building Specifications

Architect:	Marcel Breuer with Hamilton Smith
Consulting Architect:	Michael Irving
Structural Engineer:	Paul Weidlinger
Mechanical Engineers:	Werner, Jensen and Korst
Lighting Consultant:	Edison Price
Contractor:	HRH Construction Corporation
Key Dates:	Design: 1963
	Construction: 1964–66
	Inauguration: 28 September 1966
Floor Area:	Gross floor area: 82,000 square feet
	Net gallery area: 26,700 square feet
	Sculpture Court: 3,100 square feet
	Storage: 21,500 square feet
	Office space: 12,200 square feet
Gallery Height:	Fourth Floor: 17 feet, 6 inches
	Third Floor: 12 feet, 6 inches
	Second Floor:
	Main gallery: 12 feet, 10 inches
	Back galleries: 14 feet, 4½ inches
	Film/video gallery: 12 feet, 10½ inches
	Lobby gallery: 12 feet, 10½ inches

Seating Capacity:	Restaurant: 75
	Film/video gallery: 120
Lighting:	Outlets placed on tracks in grid ceiling spaced every 6 inches east to west, every 2 feet north to south.
	Fourth Floor: 250 watt quartz, 3200° K
	Other galleries: 150 watt incandescent, 2800° K
	Lighting adjusted to exhibition; no more than 12 candlepower for works on paper
Materials:	Facade: unpolished granite
	Bridge: wood-grain textured concrete
	Floors: bluestone
	Ceilings: concrete grid
	Stairs: terrazzo
	Counters: polished granite
	Bannisters: teak
	Walls: bush-hammered concrete; gallery partitions constructed as needed for exhibitions
	Elevator doors, glass frames, details: architectural bronze

Key to Photographs

*All black-and-white photographs taken by Ezra Stoller in 1966, except as noted.
All color photographs taken by Jeff Goldberg from 1999–2000, except as noted.*

Published by
Princeton Architectural Press
37 East Seventh Street
New York, NY 10003

For a catalog of books published by Princeton Architectural Press, call toll free 1.800.722.6657
or visit www.papress.com

Series editor & book design: Mark Lamster

Acknowledgments
I would like to thank my colleagues at Esto Photographics, especially Sara Armstrong, and
at TSI, Mary Milo and Margeris Kimenis, for their help in preparing these images. We are
grateful to Mark Lamster for his support of the Building Blocks series from its inception.
—Erica Stoller

This book would not have been possible without the enthusiastic support of the Whitney
Museum of American Art and its staff, in particular Maxwell L. Anderson, Mary DelMonico,
Anita Duquette, May Castleberry, and Dale Tucker. Princeton Architectural Press also
acknowledges Ann Alter, Amanda Atkins, Nicola Bednarek, Eugenia Bell, Jan Cigliano, Jane
Garvie, Caroline Green, Mia Ihara, Leslie Ann Kent, Clare Jacobson, Annie Nitschke,
Lottchen Shivers, Jennifer Thompson, and Deb Wood.—Kevin C. Lippert, publisher

For the licensing of Ezra Stoller images, contact Esto Photographics.

Printed and bound in China

Library of Congress Cataloging-in-Publication Data
Stoller, Ezra.
    Whitney Museum of American Art / photographs by Ezra Stoller;
  preface by Maxwell L. Anderson ; introduction by K. Michael Hays. -- 1st ed.
      p.   cm. -- (The building blocks series)
  Includes bibliographical references.
   ISBN 1-56898-260-7 (alk. paper)
   1. Whitney Museum of American Art--Pictorial works. 2. New York
  (N.Y.)--Buildings, structures, etc.--Pictorial works. I. Title II.
  Building Blocks series (New York, N.Y.)
   N618.S76 2000
   727'.7'097471--dc21   00-009948